The way to maturity in PHP application lifecycle

ERICO VASCONCELOS

DEDICATION

This book is dedicated to those who wish to go beyond and raise their vision on how to achieve more results from their investments in PHP by elevating maturity in the application lifecycle.

CONTENTS

INTRODUCTION

December 2013. A customer hires my company so we can support them at a critical time when their application will go-live. Access volume should rise rapidly in the first hour after the system become available to the public. I, along with some excellent professionals, find myself in a room to monitor the opening moment.

With the help of the right tools, in the past few months, we've run tests that guarantee server responsiveness for up to 3000 requests per second. The application is managed from a single centralized point, and we have the ability to identify the problems before they are pointed out by the users. Through a dashboard, we can keep track of all incidents related to application slowness, errors, and resource consumption. The user session is shared among all 30 servers through high availability. We were able to quickly identify the response time of the servers, breaking the total time between the PHP processing, the database, and the sending of traffic on the network.

At midnight, the system opens and quickly reaches 70,000 simultaneous users navigating the application. The tension rises as the number of users increases. Meanwhile, we keep a close eye on response time indicators and application errors. No problem until then. After stabilizing the number of visits during a time, the number begins to decrease, and we realize that the first peak had been successfully overcome.

Despite all the concerns regarding the risks of system problems, the client had an excellent experience and was able to reap the benefits of good maturity in relation to team knowledge, methodologies and professional tools.

For more than 11 years now, helping organizations evolve their maturity in the PHP application lifecycle has been an essential mission for my company. Situations like the one described above are moments of victory in which we see the benefits of investing in tools, methodologies and training so that we can offer services with more and more effectiveness.

In this book, I'll introduce you to what I've learned in these situations, and how you can use that knowledge to help deliver faster, less error-prone, more productive, more reliable applications.

CHAPTER 1 - THE WAY TO MATURITY IN PHP APPLICATION LIFECYCLE

Before entering the subject of the challenges of maturity, I'll share a bit about my story: how I fell in love with PHP and why I dedicated myself to helping organizations succeed with their PHP investments.

The story began in March 2000; I was 17 years old. I was in the third year of high school, and I came across the dilemma of any teen at that age: the only thing you can think of this year is the college entrance exam and what course you want to enter.

It was tricky for me, especially because, up until the previous year, I was confident on the idea of being a professional tennis player. And my expectations weren't set to be the number one in the world, like Guga or Pete Sampras (my idols then). Okay, I wanted to play ATP professional tournaments. But I planned to make the goal of being a teacher abroad possible. It was all right. However, a small detail pulled me away from this dream: I was a terrible player. It's sad, I know. But it's true. My tournament results forced me to see that, in the junior year, I should probably consider another alternative.

So, that year, I stopped training, and I dedicated myself to studying for the college entrance examination. In the first month, I suffered a lot from the lack of exercise routine, and I felt I needed to do something besides studying. Even because studying was not a very tempting idea, that way, in an ordinary afternoon, after college, utterly bored, I found myself thinking about the only thing I knew how to do that could have some value for someone: a website.

That way, I went door to door in the neighborhood, offering shopkeepers solutions on how they could sum up Geocities + HTML services to have a website. And I charged $ 40 to make the page. That was my first contact with the "professional" creation of an internet site. To this day, I have the pleasure of having an excellent relationship with Ricardo, of RIGO furniture store, my second client of that day.

In October 2003, after a few years working on maintenance and building static sites for some clients while working on a Dreamweaver project, I decided to explore their help menu. There was a little treasure that changed my life.

In the *Dreamweaver* menu, there was an explanation on how to create a connection to the MySQL database and make queries. And, with the results, you could assemble your page.

That discovery was fabulous. If you remember the first time you linked the ability of a programming language to a database, you know what I'm talking about. That powerful feeling: we think we have, in short, the tool to solve "ALL" the problems of the world; tell us a situation, we have managed to ensure that it is possible to resolve with PHP/MySQL. After a while, we realize that this is not the case, but we can, in fact, solve many issues with these tools.

Let's jump for 16 years ahead. My life today is a little different, but not so much. After that day, I did countless site projects, working for countless small businesses. I worked in a software factory, developing with a great team and with projects for large organizations. Now, with my company, I have over 10,000 hours of consulting and support, helping organizations address the major issues they encounter in the PHP application lifecycle: performance, scalability, reliability, architecture, identification, and bug fixes, productivity, among others.

I call these challenges "maturity challenges." That is because, if think about it, they will never, in fact, be solved. They are like spirals, where you can always evolve and, as advanced as you can, there can always be some way to improve.

In these years, helping organizations work with PHP, we support and help many of them overcome the barriers they encountered and evolve in their maturity curve. For this, we have created a business unit in the company, which we call "Enterprise PHP", through which our mission is to help organizations improve the results of their investments in PHP.

My purpose in this book is to reinforce this mission. It is sharing with the reader our methodology, how we have helped these organizations in more than 18 years to improve the results of their investments in PHP.

One thing I've noticed over the years is that regardless of the technology and programming language your organization chooses to work with, the factor that will be most critical to the medium- and-long-term success of your project is the level of maturity that you reaches.

That way, even though some languages may have specific advantages for solving specific tasks, most of the time, this will not make the difference in using a technology.

What will make the difference will be the maturity with which you apply concepts, tools, and methodologies throughout the application life cycle to achieve your goal.

In that way, let us think about maturity. It's not binary. Something you have or do not have. It is something that is built every day as a positive spiral, where today's achievements unlock new challenges and propel you to new levels of maturity.

When I remember the first projects, I realize how some concerns, such as productivity and performance, were already present at that time. Of course, they did not have the same level of technical challenge or relevance to the business that we meet with my clients in the future, such as enrolling students in college entrance exams, scheduling clinical appointments, or even the end-service offered by agencies credit. But somehow, they were already quite relevant concerns.

Many of the challenges that we will present in this book are not restricted to PHP. They are common in the life cycle of applications developed in any language, in PHP, Java, .NET, C #, or any other available in the market.

Furthermore, I do not intend to solve the questions presented decisively, not least because I do not believe that it is possible to achieve a definitive result. But, yes, help you to go through the main disputes that we have already encountered, present how we solved, and help you raise the level of maturity, taking you to other levels with unprecedented provocations to be experienced. I want to shorten your path and give you the tools I have today to help you succeed. And, above all, save your energy to overcome new challenges.

To demonstrate this concept, let's consider, for example, the performance of your application. You can optimize your application in order to obtain excellent performance, however, it will not come to an end. Every day, new possibilities arises, and you must continue in this endless search for optimization, building your knowledge on top of previous victories. Advances can come from evolutions, both in the application architecture, and in hardware resources that can lead to new levels of performance.

The technology itself evolves and will make us always aim for better results at all levels. See, for example, the incredible advance of the PHP language, which, from version 5.6 to 7.0, had average gains of twice the performance with the consumption of half of memoryThis incredible gain was available with the simple update of the PHP version. Isn't it amazing?

And that is not all. With the advances made in Zend's labs in optimizing the engine with the use of the compiled version of PHP, we will probably have incredible performance gains in version 8 as well, just by updating the PHP version. A preview of what is to come has already been presented with the JIT compiler, which will allow incredible gains in highly processed scripts. In any case, this book is intended to assist you in understanding some solutions that can lead you to take a step forward in several of the issues we will be addressing. These advances can impel you and your organization to save a lot of investment in time and effort to resolve these deadlocks. If I can help you overcome a critical challenge that your company encounters, I will have achieved my goal.

Let's start with a classic challenge: getting the operation and development teams to work together!

CHAPTER 2 - DEVOPS

For successful software development, we have to ensure that everyone involved is working together for the success of the project. The life cycle of a PHP application begins with the development team, passes through the test team, and then reaches the stage of going into production. At this time, there is a need for joint work between the team responsible for ensuring a safe and performing production environment and the one that developed the application.

Making these teams work together is not always an easy task. So, make that happen, we need to understand how these teams work.

The routine of the development and operations teams is already quite agitated by itself.

Development teams need to deal with design methodologies, frameworks, data modeling, system modeling, code production, test writing, and countless other daily activities necessary to achieve their goals.

Operational teams, on the other hand, need to deal with several other challenges to keep the operation running smoothly, involving security, connectivity, configurations of environments, operating systems, firewalls, among many other problems.

These routines are already quite challenging for both teams on a day to day basis. At some times, however, they need to work together whether to launch a software version, to improve performance, or to identify the root cause of problems that are occurring in production.

If the organization does not have adequate maturity in place to make this works, it may lead to a losing game. In some situations, it can lead to severe conflicts and "push games" of responsibility.

However, proper maturity enables teamwork that can lead to excellent results for all. Clarity of objectives, constant review, and people engaged in collaboration are critical for everyone to work towards the same goal.

The objective is to deliver the application with a minimum impact as possible. As the speed of development progresses, the need for fast deliveries has become a necessity in virtually every team.

In this context, the concept of continuous delivery arises, which is the ability to deliver new versions of the software routinely, with a high frequency. We can achieve that by gaining the ability to automate the steps required to put the application in the air.

The range of tools for continuous delivery automation has evolved a great deal in recent years. Continuous delivery is a concept that has developed in conjunction with agile development methodologies that have required a consistent way of ensuring that the source code leaves the development stage for the final production environment.

From Jenkins to Gitlab, several tools can work together to create the necessary sequence of delivery. To this sequence, we call the Pipeline. In these steps, we can perform several actions, such as software versioning, quality checks, performance checks, security checks, code packaging, permissions settings. These steps take the sequence until we lead the application to the final environment, and it is available for users to use.

This concept is behind the main tools of continuous delivery automation. Once you understand and design the ideal Pipeline for your application, adopting a software becomes a much more straightforward job.

There is no ideal Pipeline, it reflects the level of maturity that you seek to have in your deliveries. In its simplest case, we usually find only the checkout of the source code from its repository and the copy to the production environment.

From this primary sequence, you can increment with additional steps. One of the first steps you might want to automate is configuring your application with production resource data (such as a database) and permissions. Additionally, you can evolve with increased performance, safety, and quality checks.

The configuration of your web server is one of the crucial steps. Depending on which server you are using, you can do this in a variety of ways.

Let's consider, for example, that you are using Apache. You can configure it using your default folder (htdocs), or create a virtual host (virtual host) file for your application.

In this scenario, you will have to manage this manually. However, there are professional tools on the market that can help you with this task. Let's check, for example, how Zend Server can help with this activity.

Using Zend Server allows you to deliver your software in an incredibly simple way, such as a drag and drop (from Zend Studio), or even a click of a button (from the interface Zend Server) or an API (a line of code for use in automation).

This capability is the end of the need to manipulate Apache files manually.

How does Zend Server deliver the software?

Zend Server will manipulate Apache files by automating this activity and reducing its need to manage Apache files manually.

Even though Zend Server does this automatically, let's understand how it handles the Apache configuration files under the hook.

Before we start, we have to understand a bit about how the Apache configuration works.

Apache has a fundamental configuration file that can have some names, depending on your version of the operating system. This file is usually apache.conf or httd.conf.

In this file, we have the basic server settings, such as the root path of the server and the overwrite permissions.

However, one of Apache's powers is the ability to extend this configuration by adding new configuration files to the original file; and by setting rules for smaller scopes.

By including a new configuration file, these are consolidated, forming a single source of rules, as well as the possibility of adding new configuration files. Apache also allows you to include configuration files to a separate folder through the .htaccess file.

This file defines more restrictive rules than general ones. That way, you have a macro rule that can be extended by new files.

This capability is hugely exploited by Zend Server when manipulating Apache files and provides a complete and straightforward structure to operate.

Zend Server creates a folder structure for the applications that will run on the server. For each new system, you will have a specific folder in that structure for the configuration file (under "/usr/local/zend/etc/sites.d") and a root folder for your own source code (under "/usr/local/zend/var/apps").

By taking care of the configuration step of your web server for you, Zend Server makes this one less issue to worry and, at the same time, provides a configuration pattern for your organization.

Another popular tool to enable its continuous delivery is Jenkins.

Jenkins is an open-source software tool that was derived from the Hudson project when Oracle acquired it. You can install the Java package in your Windows, Mac OS X or Linux environment and run the service.

Its philosophy is to create steps that will compose all the activities necessary for the code to leave its repository to the production environment. To create the steps, you can use a variety of ways, such as build tools, plug-ins provided for specific tools, or even merely shell commands.

One of the significant challenges of implementing a strategy of automation of delivery in organizations is related to the traditional separation between development and production. This challenge is one of the main obstacles to be able to increase the maturity of DevOps work.

Since delivery requires the involvement of both parties, any strategy that is performed exclusively by one of the parties will be fragile and will lack critical information about the process.

The involvement of both parties has led organizations to demand teams and professionals who are knowledgeable about the realities of both sides to create a more harmonious and efficient flow.

Zend has also expanded its elegant solution to cover one of the most common conflicts between the parties in delivering the answers: the packaging of the application.

When assessing how teams communicate, it has been found that application requirements are often passed on in failed documentation. It may involve extensions dependencies, PHP configurations, compatibilities, among others.

The ZPK solution was a simple way that – when creating a .xml file (called deployment.xml) containing metadata about the project – the development team can write all the dependencies, compatibilities, requirements and other information about the application and delivered along with the project in an XML file, which is stored in the repository itself along with the app.

If you package your application with this file and upload it to Zend Server, it will take care of the magic of configuring your server.

The package consists of at least the deployment.xml file and the files in your application. Is made a .zip compression (Zend's pick is by extension zpk, but it's a compressed file anyhow) it's ready. It is possible to further elaborate this package by including scripts to run on specific steps on the server, but in its basic configuration, it is straightforward.

It is because, as we saw earlier, Zend Server manages the configuration of your web server for you, reducing your need to worry.

However, eventually, it may be necessary to have manual interventions, so it is good that you know how "magic" works.

When placing an application on a server, you will have at least two significant steps: copying the files and configuring your web server.

In regards to copying the files, we have seen that Zend Server will create a structure inside the /usr/local/zend/var/apps (in Linux environments) folder. For each delivery, a new folder containing a complete version of your application will be created.

Zend Server will always keep the last and the penultimate versions; this is to ensure that you have the possibility of an easy rollback in case of need.

In the past, Zend Server changed the configuration file to point the application to the new folder created in delivery. Still, in its newer versions, it started to perform a symbolic link pointing through the operating system.

That way, for the web server configuration, the directory is always the same. What happens is that the operating system points the "official" directory to the created one during the deployment process.

Already in the configuration stage of the webserver, you will have different procedures in case of using Apache or Nginx. Consider Apache.

Apache has a cascading configuration structure, which allows, in general, a global configuration to be overwritten by a more localized configuration for just one application. Yes, it is possible to prevent a setting from being overwritten, but consider this a truth for pedagogical purposes.

Zend Server has added a few lines at the end of the Apache configuration to include all configuration files located inside the Zend Server folder (/usr/local/zend/etc/).

With this, it was able to take responsibility for managing these files and simplified the work of publishing an application on an Apache server.

Now, from the Zend Server interface itself, you can create a new virtual server directly, and let Zend Server manipulate the files for you. It will create the data within its folder. It will not be a problem since the folder is set up, as mentioned above.

In addition to allowing you to deploy your application efficiently and visually, Zend Server also brings a robust API with commands that will enable you to do virtually everything you do manually, however, via the shell.

This API is a powerful ally in your journey towards automating seamless delivery because it is used within a stage of your Pipeline to ensure the deployment of the application to the final production environment.

In recent years, the continuous delivery scenario is one with the most advanced rithm of inovations. Excellent tools have elevated the number of possibilities you have to automate the steps.

Many of them do the same thing, so it's essential to think of your Pipeline fairly consistently to avoid it from generating unnecessary automation to take advantage of the capabilities of the tools.

Remember that sometimes less is more, and in automation, it is always the best to think about what you want to do first.

It is worth mentioning the significant advance that the container world has brought to computing. The speed and utilization of the resources generated by the container solutions is a fantastic thing that already affects and will significantly affect, in a significant way, the way we do things in the future.

The use of containers in a continuous delivery solution is also widely discussed, mainly because of the ability to deliver to the developer an environment equal to what will be executed in production.

However, once again, even if you use the strategy of promoting a development container to production environment, you still have to worry about several issues we discussed earlier, such as the PHP .ini files, permissions, database, storage notes, among others.

So at some point, you'll have to think about your Pipeline and how you will take care of the delivery.

The most important thing about knowing the potential tools is to ensure that you know how to use the most appropriate tool for your scenario. Therefore, start slowly with the minimum and plan the evolution, always analyzing the reason for each decision.

Now let's talk about a central theme: performance.

CHAPTER 3 - APPLICATION PERFORMANCE

Everyone wants fast applications. And the best thing is that the concept of 'fast' is quite volatile. After all, every day, we work with more powerful computers, more efficient programming languages, and more advanced capabilities for software development.

In the same way, we are also advancing the capabilities we want to build, advancing the barriers of technologies with features that require more resources and processing. This reality holds for audio, video, artificial intelligence, and many borders that were previously unthinkable.

Dealing with application performance is a game you can never win. Do not get me wrong; I do not want to discourage you. I say this because there is no end. You can always improve.

This feature requires that we take a precise and systematic approach to performance because we need to have a clear comparative basis for us to evolve. Thus, any performance improvement exercise requires control of variables to isolate the improvement attempt around a variable. After all, the same application will behave differently on computers and in configurations many different.

Using the right tools can help you identify bottlenecks in your applications.

Let's take a classic example of a PHP request. Let's see what happens:

1- A visitor requests the website via browser.
2- The request arrives at the destination where it finds a load balancer. It checks the headers and forwards it to the application server.
3. Upon reaching the application server, the server checks the extension and realizes that the load balancer is routing it to a web server.
4- That way, it passes the request to the PHP engine. The engine reads the file and passes it on for static code analysis. This analysis is called PARSE, and, soon after, it is sent to execution.
5- The code, after converted into ready language, is then executed by the PHP engine.
6- During execution, it may be necessary to have external queries, mainly due to the functions related to database and web services.
7- After running, the PHP engine returns the request to the web server, which returns it to the client.

In analyzing the above steps, we can see that performance-related issues must have as a first step the identification of the moment to be optimized.

For example, for step one, where the browser submits the request to the server, it is already possible to identify optimization possibilities at this stage.

One of the possibilities would be precisely the configuration of the use of browser cache. You, as the system manager, can instruct on how the client cache will work. You can make these instructions by changing the response headers.

An example Apache configuration:
EXPIRES CACHING
<IfModule mod_expires.c>
ExpiresActive On
ExpiresByType image / jpg "access 1 year"
ExpiresByType image / jpeg "access 1 year"
ExpiresByType image / gif "access 1 year"
ExpiresByType image / png "access 1 year"
ExpiresByType text / css "access 1 month"
ExpiresByType text / html "access 1 month"
ExpiresByType application / pdf "access 1 month"
ExpiresByType text / x-javascript "access 1 month"
ExpiresByType application / x-shockwave-flash "access 1 month"
ExpiresByType image / x-icon "access 1 year"

ExpiresDefault "access 1 month"
</ IfModule>

In the example above, .htaccess was used on an Apache web server so that it includes, in the response header, instructions so that the client browser does not make unnecessary additional requests for site presentation.

Much of the browser cache settings are very difficult for you to have some control over. Precisely because it can not guarantee that actions that occur on the client-side are planned, at the end of the day, the user will have control over it.

The tip above is just an attempt to influence. However, the client must enable the browser for the use of the cache.

When we go in the path of the request to the server-side, we have new possibilities for optimizations.

Let's see, for example, what happens when a request for a PHP file arrives at Apache.

Apache verifies that the file extension is a PHP format. In this way, it passes the same to a module that will interpret the script.

The first step the PHP engine will perform is the parsing of the script. At this stage, he is only interested in static code validation to identify if there are syntax failures. This validation is essential because it prevents the script from running with typos. It is an important filter that anticipates potential issues that would prevent the code from executing as desired. After validation, the PHP engine generates another intermediate code in memory, which is then effectively run by the PHP engine.

Every time you run a PHP script, those validation steps are executed. Although very important and useful, make this validation does not make much sense if there are no changes to the code. After all, once the static validation has passed successfully, if there has been no change, it will always pass.

But PHP does this anyway. That is if the OPCache extension is not enabled. Precisely, the OPCache extension will be an essential ally to keep PHP from doing this unnecessary step.

The OPCache derives from the OPCode cache. That is the name given to an operation code, which will make your computer's processor work. In the case of PHP, it is the intermediate code after static validation. Until the early versions of PHP 5, you could choose among some alternatives to implement intermediate code caching in PHP. The main options that existed were Zend

Optimizer + and APC.

As of PHP version 5.5, Zend's OPCache extension (formerly Optimizer +) is fully incorporated into the PHP version, so if you use a higher version than this, you already have this feature available in your environment.

To enable it, make sure it is enabled in PHP.ini:

```
[opcache]
; opcache.enable = 0
; opcache.enable_cli = 0
; opcache.memory_consumption = 64
; opcache.interned_strings_buffer = 4
; opcache.max_accelerated_files = 2000
; opcache.max_wasted_percentage = 5
; opcache.use_cwd = 1
; opcache.validate_timestamps = 1
; opcache.revalidate_freq = 2
; opcache.revalidate_path = 0
; opcache.save_comments = 1
; opcache.load_comments = 1
; opcache.fast_shutdown = 0
; opcache.enable_file_override = 0
; opcache.optimization_level = 0xffffffff
; opcache.inherited_hack = 1
; opcache.dups_fix = 0
; opcache.blacklist_filename =
; opcache.max_file_size = 0
; opcache.consistency_checks = 0
; opcache.force_restart_timeout = 180
; opcache.error_log =
; opcache.log_verbosity_level = 1
; opcache.preferred_memory_model =
; opcache.protect_memory = 0
```

Using OPCache can have a major impact on the system and ensure incredible performance gains with no code changes. Let's look at some settings:

```
opcache.validate_timestamps = 1
```

This setting asks if we want the timestamp of the script file to be queried. This check is important if you want the cached version not to be used after a change to the original script.

If you turn off this option, we have to be careful about new system updates. That's because we will not see the latest changes while clearing the OPCache cache.

For this, the timestamp ensures that the opcache always verifies the metadata of the file. If you have a deployment process that ensures that the cache is cleared and you do not do this often, it may be worth putting the value to 0 and preventing this unnecessary step from being performed.

; opcache.max_accelerated_files

This variable is also very useful. Because, if we have a very reliable project, we may not have put all scripts in the cache. Of course, we have to make sure we have the resources available for this, but if we do, we can have a potential performance improvement by ensuring that we have all the files set to cache.

; opcache.memory_consumption = 64

This variable also helps our configuration a lot. It defines the maximum size of shared memory that will be allocated for OPCache. If we have available resources, this value may be limiting the potential use of the cache. So it's worth checking it out.

While using OPCache can bring gains of up to 2-3 times, our journey towards performance gain does not have to stop here. We will follow the flow of the request and deal with one of the main alternatives for performance gain, the Data Cache.

Data Cache is, without a doubt, one of the most flexible and compelling alternatives to gaining performance in your application. By identifying the piece of code responsible for the performance bottleneck, you can see if it is a viable candidate for data cache usage.

For this, you need to check how critical it is that your data are in real-time. If your code queries the database, queries a web service, or performs a complex math operation, you need to check whether this result needs to be in real-time or if you can have a time window in which the data may be reused by following requests.

Consider a scenario where a system queries an external web service to fetch customer relationship data. Let's suppose now that this query always takes more than 2 seconds, and this is directly impacting the performance of your system.

The first step would be to identify whether this relationship needs to be always current, or if you have a time window (for example, 30 min) so that the list is updated.

In our case, we can not identify this response with only the information we have but check on your system. Sometimes we believe that we always need to have real-time data, and we do not even check it out.

We can also have cases where the need for renewing the cached data is not related to time rather than new action. For example, in our specific case, we may be able to receive the same list every time, indefinitely, unless there is a new customer.

The use of data caching gives us great flexibility because we can define what we want to cache, how long, where and also we can clear the cache when an event occurs manually.

This set of possibilities is quite powerful for us to use in our systems and can, therefore, reduce the time of entire requests from seconds to a few milliseconds.

The concept of data caching follows the following logic:

- 1) It tries to fetch the data in a data cache in a certain location. (Eg zend_shm_cache_fetch)
- 2) If you can not return anything, it is because it does not exist; in this way, it executes the complete code.
- 3) After executing the code, save the result to a data cache in a certain location (e.g., zend_shm_cache_store).

This simple logic is enhanced with features for clearing cache, such as by calling the zend_shm_cache_delete function (in case of using Zend Server as the backend).

This function can be called after another part of the application to clear the cache. For example, you could call it after the insert of a new record to ensure the cache is rebuilt the next request.

One of the most exciting things about data caching is that we rarely see in blogs and books the information that sometimes the data cache is no more performative than the original code.

It may seem a little contradictory to understand that data caching is no longer performative. It is because you will only place the data cache if it is faster; otherwise, you keep the code executed manually.

Great, you're right. The problem, however, is that this may not appear on a system with few accesses. An exemplary case is when we load a very large resultset into the data cache.

Querying the data cache can be much faster than querying the database. But as our system grows, the memory usage and access volume might bring the cost of data caching too high. In that case, you might find yourself in a situation where the access time to the data cache as being responsible for the bottleneck of your application.

One way to identify this situation is to use Zend Server's Code Tracing. With it, you can check exactly which part of your application is generating the bottleneck.

In our example, one output would remove the data cache from the whole table and put an index in the query so that instead of using the cache, the user would go to the database but with the specific index.

I know it may sound unbelievable, but believe me. This information can help you unlock the performance of high-load critical applications.

Okay, we've already checked the browser cache setting, the opcode cache, and the data cache. What else can we check to improve the performance of our application?

Our next step would be to check the possibility of using the page cache. This solution is one of the main alternatives for improving performance. In its principle, when adopting a page cache, we skipped all the processing of the script, and we returned the result of previous processing that was saved for that purpose.

For this reason, page caching will undoubtedly bring in incredible gains for your application. However, one of the main problems with page caching is that it can only be used if you are not using pages with variable content. And in systems, this is almost always true. This way, it is complicated to skip the processing of a script and take advantage of the previous output.

However, there are some cases that we can escape from a superficial analysis of the situation. That's because sometimes the only thing that changes is a small part. Consider the case of a news portal. In some cases, the only difference between the public and personalized version is the user information on the screen.

In a preliminary analysis, we could consider that this page could not be cached since it contains data from the logged in users.

However, an exit would be the use of additional asynchronous requests for the dynamic part of the page and the use of page cache for the static part of the site.

In this way, for a logged-in user, we would load the cached version of the page in the original request. This version contains only content that is served to everyone. And, via javascript, we trigger a new request that returns only the user data and rewrites the page by inserting the dynamic information.

It is a powerful way to improve the performance of our application.

Solutions for page caching can be numerous and implemented in several ways. Various load balancing appliances have powerful capabilities for deploying this kind of solution.

There are also software-based resolutions, such as Squid, Nginx or Apache itself.

Zend Server also offers the possibility of adopting the page cache. One of its main advantages is the flexibility of establishing rules in which a cached page should be served.

Let's look at a case. Let's consider that, in the case of the virtual store that we mentioned above, you want to implement a fast cache rule for the home page. However, although it is possible to deploy versions to the page when a user is logged in, you would now only want to ensure that the version for non-logged in users is showing up in the cache.

That way, with Zend Server, you have access to PHP variables, like $ _SESSION, to use in your cache rule. That way, you mark that it will only show the page when the variable is populated with data from your client.

This ease of creating rules based on global variables is a powerful resource that can facilitate the improvement of important parts of your application.

It is always worth mentioning that the use of cache is delicate. If you implement a wrong rule, you may compromise sensitive business and customer information. So testing and reviewing these rules is never too much.

Following our assessment of performance improvements, we have found that by having opcache, cache data, and page cache in our toolkit, we are prepared to address each performance improvement scenario with fantastic tools for better results.

But we still have some other alternatives. When thinking about performance improvement, we are thinking of improving the user experience. We want it not to wait while using our system. For this reason, in addition to enhancing performance itself, we can also introduce the concept of improved responsiveness.

Responsiveness is the time the customer receives a response to a request. It may be that this response is not yet the end, but rather a transient response. That way, we keep him from waiting too long.

This scenario can occur when, to process a customer order, we have to execute a series of sequential steps that may end up demanding a high time.

If we do not give answers about processing within a given time to the customer, he may be frustrated with his experience and sometimes even cancel his operations.

This problem can be solved by breaking the linear processing sequence and by putting some steps for asynchronous processing. It is what happens when we buy a plane ticket in a company.

When we enter our credit card data, the verification of the same does not happen in the same request as the purchase confirmation. On the confirmation screen, we received only one indication that the card was registered and that the carrier will confirm the payment with the credit card operator.

This asynchronous processing does not improve performance; after all, the card verification step continues. What it does is enhance the perception of performance by the user, because the user receives a faster response indicating that the same will be verified and then receives confirmation.

That way, at some moments in our application, it may be challenging to improve the performance of some parts. Still, we have the alternative of verifying if it is possible to apply asynchronous processing.

Zend Server facilitates asynchronous processing through the Job Queue solution. This solution provides an API that allows your application to include new Jobs for asynchronous processing. The API provides a vast amount of resources available for both the creation of jobs and the management of queues.

In its WEB interface, Zend Server also offers deep visibility of what is happening with your Jobs queue. You can see how many jobs there are, what their statuses are, how they were output from each run, and how to stop and resume running them.

This solution is also beneficial for scenarios where we have peak access to the application. Because we can delegate a portion of the processing, if any, to another time, in which the system is not with a significant load. This result can be achieved easily and directly through the solution API.

Managing application performance can be quite exhausting

work, and identifying the strategy to be appropriate can be quite challenging. With the use of proper tools, we can significantly reduce efforts in the pursuit of continuous improvement in performance.

Another tool that can help a lot in this challenge is Blackfire. A profiler created by SensioLabs that allows the creation of performance tests. The concept is similar to unit tests that use statements to be confirmed and, if they are not, they present the error.

In the case of Blackfire, you can create performance assertions, such as execution time for the request and functions. You can also check the amount of execution of certain functions on the page. The profiler is simple to use and features a wealth of information that can significantly help build the arsenal for the pursuit of excellence in PHP.

Performance is one of my favorite subjects. However, we need to move forward on our journey. Let's talk about another issue that affects us in everyday life: correction of bugs.

CHAPTER 4 - IDENTIFICATION AND CORRECTION OF BUGS

Identifying and correcting bugs fast is a significant challenge for any development team. The cost of detecting a production error is far higher than identifying it at an early stage of development.

For this reason, having tools that allow you to detect errors at an early stage of development is extremely important.

For this reason, Zend created Z-Ray. Z-Ray allows the developer to identify issues in the code that could lead to higher bugs in the future.

The tool was designed with some goals in mind:

– Do not change the way developers work.

The developer's development cycle is basically to write the code in an editor, save and open the browser and press F5. This straightforward cycle is one of the greatest powers of the PHP language. In this way, any tool that would change this cycle would bring an adoption cost that could not be met by the developers.

– Anticipate as much as possible potential problems that may generate errors in production.

The Z-Ray bar has a rich set of information about the request, see:

- Page Requests – Check the requests sent to your page on the server, see your response time, methods, path, and the runtime that they had.

- Event Monitoring – used with Zend Server, event monitoring gives the visibility of events generated from the request.
- Errors and Warnings – you no longer need to open the log file to see which errors were generated. With the bug and warnings tab, you have access while browsing. And even if errors are suppressed, so they do not appear in the logs, you'll still be able to see them in Z-Ray.
- Database queries – slow queries, runtime, and a set of other information regarding queries. It show the actual versions that were run, not the one in "prepared" statements.

Z-Ray is quite powerful in its default setting. However, its capacity for growth and extension makes it one of the complete tools for the day-to-day programmer.

Zend Server features a gallery with several plug-ins available for you to use as soon as you install Z-Ray. Those plug-ins add capabilities that provides information about the architecture of leading frameworks on the market, such as Zend Framework, Laravel, Symfony. It also has information about CMS and other systems, such as WordPress. Infrastructure features like OpCache, Amazon Web Services are also present.

Also, you can also expand Z-Ray with your extensions. It can be very useful when your application has its own architectural features, such as an event system or even plug-ins.

Creating Z-Ray plug-ins can allow you to view architectural information quickly and transparently while browsing the application. Ever wondered how much time you can save on your team when figuring out possible mistakes?

Now, when mistakes happen in production, the problem is more serious. A bug can generate an incalculable business risk. Depending on the application, it can lead to financial losses or even damage to the organization's image.

However, without the right tools, teams often do not know how to identify the root cause. Except for application and PHP logs, it is challenging to have something else to help identify the root cause.

Without an adequate tool to assist, some teams use the approach to try to replicate the problem in development environment to generate hypotheses to try to solve the issues.

The drawback is that it is not always easy to replicate the error. The team may have to work a lot more (not infrequently, outside business hours, or on weekends) and still can not solve it.

The problem is that production variables are not always replicable; the same database status, access volume, and information passed by users can be complicated to replicate.

With Zend Server, you gain visibility into the environment in terms of events. When a particular event, whether related to performance, resource consumption, or even errors, happens in your application, an event will be generated, letting you know before the phone rings.

Another fantastic thing about monitoring is that it comes with context information: environment, session, request, and back-trace variables. This information eliminates much of the need to try to replicate the problem that occurred.

By already having all the context and event information, teams can have the root cause much more easily without having to spend the energy and time to replicate the problem.

Those capabilities allows them to focus their energies on solving the problem and to use their knowledge in the search for creative solutions that can fix the issue.

In addition to monitoring and contextual information, Zend Server also has a feature called Code Tracing. It is the black box of your request. By black box, we are saying that it will record everything that happened in fact at the request of your user who generated the event.

The level of detail is incredible, even presenting the execution time, the memory consumption, parameters, and returns of all the functions executed in the due request.

This feature has an advanced debugging level, and when enabled, will provide you with all the information you need to understand what happened to a particular request: both the sequence of functions and their memory and time consumption, along with their variables and their outputs. Without a doubt, the complete information you will get about your request.

The drawback is that there is a cost to register this information, so you will not want to keep it on at all times. Ideally, you should only keep in stand-by mode, so that it will only be activated when a certain event occurs.

In addition to these tools, you can also count on an APM solution to provide a look at other assets and measure user perception. Its main difference with the information provided by Zend Server is precisely in monitoring issues outside the application, such as the database and the networks. These are questions that can directly aid the user's perception.

In the next chapter we will address an issue that has generated much interest today: scalability.

CHAPTER 5 - SCALABILITY

Scalability is a beautiful problem to have. If you're concerned with scalability, it means that your solution is helping a lot of people and that, to meet more, you need to resolve that issue.

There are many issues involved in scalability, the technical difficulty is just one of them, and the costs and procedural feasibility are equally challenging.

In recent times, several solutions have been developed, allowing more and more to work with automated provisioning. Cloud solutions such as Azure, AWS and Google Cloud, among others, have made it easy for everyone to have access to virtually unlimited capabilities and scalability, of course, tied to the ability to pay for it.

Automated provisioning solutions, however, will not always work out for you. In the case of your PHP applications, sometimes you have to ensure that all applications are available on new servers, that the extensions are the same, and that this situation does not change over time.

When addressing the issue of the scalability in PHP applications, we have to separate some topics. The first of these is the automation of infrastructure. The second is PHP itself.

This separation is essential, mainly due to the advance of cloud computing solutions. Concepts such as self-provision, elasticity, self-service, on-demand, resilience, and pool of resources were presented to the world by providers. This new reality raised to another level the supply of computational capacity to all organizations.

Self-provisioning is the ability to automatically add computing power to an environment by reaching a particular metric. For example, add more HTTP servers whenever it reaches a load of 60. This capability allows a given environment to match demand automatically.

This concept is tied to elasticity, which is the capacity for the expansion of an environment. To have the ability to be self-provisioned, you need elasticity first.

With cloud offerings, we also have access to computing capacity on a self-service basis. When we need it, it will be available. When we do not need it, turn it off. And all accessible through a self-service dashboard over the internet.

These computational resources are universal and serve the underlying infrastructure for hosting a PHP application. However, for language, we have some issues that are specific and that we will have to solve independently of the infrastructure we will adopt.

These issues are centralized configuration, deploy, audit trail, and session cluster.

To help with these challenges, we have several ways to do and to help. Let's review how Apache works, then introduce some features of Zend Server and how it can support them in these impasses.

When we mention about the centralized configuration, we are referring to the PHP and webserver config. Regardless of the webserver you choose, you will need to configure in a way it can serve your application correctly.

You will also have to configure PHP so that it has all the appropriate settings for the security, performance, and operation of your application.

If you are using Apache, you will notice that it uses a configuration file to store all its settings. In some environments, it is apache.conf; in others, it is httpd.conf.

This file has several relevant directives, but I'll highlight DocumentRoot and the Directory settings. The first one is responsible for mapping the root folder of your web server. When accessing your web server, this is the first folder that will be displayed.

However, Apache can expand its settings file through the use of "includes". These "includes" allows you to append other files to the main config and make it behave as if they were all a single large file.

This way, you may have other .conf files that are being included inside Apache and may override or expand the "default" settings.

One of the characteristics responsible for Apache server versatility is the ability to host multiple contexts within a single server through the use of VirtualHost tag. On a virtual host, you can add new root paths to new server names. Also, all configuration, such as the port that will listen to (Listen tag) and the directory configuration (by the Directory tag).

This capability allows you to host multiple applications with different URLs on a single server through a separate configuration file for each and consolidated in the Apache configuration file.

Zend Server expands this Apache expand capability by adding a new folder structure to the Apache configuration file.

By using "Includes", Zend Server adds all files with the .conf extension located in the /usr/local/zend/etc/sites.d folder as part of the Apache configuration file. And set the /usr/local/zend/var/apps folder as the root for deploying all applications.

Let's consider now an example of an application hosted in 60 servers. How to ensure that every host has the same settings? I know there are numerous tools for automation that simplify setting up multiple environments from a single location.

Tools like Ansible make this task extremely simple. If you do not use one of these tools, you will have to do them manually and this can be very difficult.

Now, the main challenge of configuration is not to make everything the same and, yes, to keep everything the same during the time. Sometimes, at first, you make all the settings and make sure that all new servers come up with the same configuration.

And then? How to ensure that, after three weeks or 3 years, no one has changed a setting on a particular server? What if your application is intermittently running exactly because a server is misconfigured? How do you find this information?

At the moment, owning a professional tool can save you a lot of time. Zend Server creates a copy of your configuration and saves it to the server. Every 30 seconds, it queries a particular server that tells back how its configuration is. Then, Zend Server compares the two information and alerts if they are not identical.

This warning can help you save days in time to search for production errors that are a consequence of inaccurate configuration.

In addition to this protection, Zend Server also offers a very intuitive interface for changing PHP configuration variables. You can do everything centralized, and it will take care of applying to all servers. Settings on the virtual host can also be made this way.

This functionality is also handy when adding or removing new computers to a cluster. Zend Server will copy Apache's PHP and virtual server settings to the new server, ensuring that it is aligned with the cluster configuration.

This ability to manipulate the server configuration led Zend Server to simplify and standardize one of the main tasks of infrastructure management for PHP: the configuration after the deployment of a new version.

To get an application up and running, you need to go through two stages: the first is to copy the files to the root directory of the application; the second is the virtual server configuration to ensure that your application will work.

Zend Server performs the two activities for you. Just upload the application package, which will take care of these steps.

Only for pedagogical purposes, and although we have covered superficially in chapter 1, we will dive into more detail on this process.

Zend Server has the concept of application packaging that represents the compression of application files with a file and configuration folders for creating a new virtual server.

This package has a skeleton that contains a deployment.xml file, which stores all of the application's meta-information. In this file, the following information is defined:

- Appdir. It is the XML tag that contains the folder where the files are in the package structure;
- Name, summary, and version with package metadata;
- Scriptsdir. This HTML tag is responsible for containing the folder where there may be PHP files that run at a particular time in the deployment.

Every time you install a PHP application using Zend Deployment, it performs the following steps:

- It will unzip and copy the package files to the

31

/usr/local/zend/var/apps/http/$__default__/0/$system /$1.0.0_$1 folder. The variable part of the folder path will be filled based on the information specific to your application.

- It will configure the virtual host file, defined in /usr/local/zend/etc/sites.d/$sistema.conf, with the variable part of the folder path will be defined specifically for your application.

In case of upgrading an existing application, Zend Server will ensure that you always have two versions of your application available on your server's disk.

This ensures that in case of need to roll back your application, it can be done in a fast, reliable way. In previous versions, this action was performed by changing the document root in the virtual server configuration file (vhost). However, in the latest versions, this is already being done based on a symbolic link, and in vhost there is a path that is a symbolic link to the actual path of the latest version. If you have to go back to the previous version, Zend Server will change the symbolic link back to the previous folder. That won't generate any stops in any Zend service.

Let's move on to one of the other significant challenges when using a web application in PHP and especially when we are going to scale: the availability of session files.

To make sure we're on the same page, let's do a quick review of the concept of sessions in PHP. Web applications have evolved a lot in front end programming, and nowadays, they basically do not need user session files because they perform backend requests just to search for specific data.

However, until a few days ago, the architecture of PHP applications passed mainly through the MVC architecture and the server-side processing of the system output in HTML. Although this architecture has evolved a lot, it may still be necessary to deal with this challenge in its applications.

The session file is responsible for keeping server-side browsing session information in your application on the server-side. If it is a virtual store with the session file, you guarantee that the visitor can make several requests to visit products while browsing your application and will always keep a single set of data valid for all navigation, such as the cart of shopping.

This was a brilliant solution that allowed the emergence

of countless services and products in our economy that have altered our society worldwide.

However, this capability also raises a big question that we have to deal with when we take care of our application: where will we store session data while our visitors navigate our application?

The PHP standard is to use the so-called "files". A fairly simple and efficient strategy that adopts a directory on your computer, usually within the /tmp folder, and starts saving the session data from the visitor to a file.

PHP calls the backend the place where we keep guest sessions. There are numerous backends, and you can change them by changing the variable session.save_handler, available in your PHP.INI.

And, if "files" solution does so well, why do we have to worry about it in an environment of scalability?

Because the "files" do not serve clustered environments well, the "files" is composed of a single folder on the operating server. This way, you would need to ensure that regardless of which server to receive the visitor's request, it will be possible to retrieve user session data and respond to the request.

Let's look at the following alternatives to the backend of the session files: database, files, Memcache and Zend Server.

It is essential to understand that, from a work/don't work perspective, all solutions will do the job.

So, the approach we will use towards those solutions will be related to the high-availability of the session information and the workload to maintain.

The high-availability is important because if we lose the session info, the user will be kicked from our site, and that could represent a business loss. The workload to maintain is essential because it is directly associated with the total cost of ownership of the solution.

The database is an interesting solution. It is meant to high load, so will be a good fit to handle the traffic load. The high-availability criteria is also able to handle, as most database engines do offer HA solution. The main issue with the database approach to handling user sessions is the overhead on managing the DBMS that could arise.

The other solution is "files". As we mentioned, "files" is the default solution for a single server environment. When considering files to cluster environments, we will need to make the folder available for network traffic to make sure the resource is available throwout the servers. The use of a network file system or even a faster file solution like a storage area network will solve the technical challenge of shared sessions. The overhead to manage distributed files approach towards user sessions won't be a big issue, but when we talk about high-availability, the performance issue to deal with the files could affect drastically the end-user experience.

The use of Memcache is also a good alternative. Once again, if we look through the HA and management perspective, we will also have the overhead in management, as we will add another server to monitor and manage. Additionally, Memcache does not provide high-availability as a standard feature, although, it is possible to add a high-availability layer to Memcache. This will add one more asset to plan and sustain. If you build a cluster of Memchace servers, they will growth the total capacity of the cluster, but if you lose a server, you will end losing the sessions recorded on that section of the cluster.

Zend Server approach is composed of an elegant solution by adding an HA layer to the "files" solution. All session files are stored in the local "files" repository. To handle the availability of session information throughout the cluster, the Zend Server Session daemon handles the communication of session data in the cluster. So if a server that doesn't have the session file of a request needs to have access to the session information, the daemon will reach out to the server to get the information. The HA is accomplished by storing a copy of the session file in a backup server in the cluster, so you will always have a copy of the session in two servers of your cluster. This solution will handle management overhead, the high-availability and the performance of session query in a very elegant way, providing a substantial benefit over other approaches.

For this reason, Zend Server will be an excellent tool to help in automated provisioning as it will take care of these issues of deployment, PHP configuration, and session of your application.

The issues we raise in this chapter may not have a great deal of technical complexity and can be solved in a number of manual ways. However, the point we are dealing with is precisely the rise of maturity. Deployment, configuration management, and session are items that can bring a lot of headaches if they are not properly treated; and especially as we seek to grow our service capacity, it is crucial to have reliable ways to handle these demands. We can save a lot of time and work with the right tools.

Scalability is undoubtedly a hot topic. In the next chapter, we will abort the question of productivity.

CHAPTER 6 - PRODUCTIVITY

Productivity is one of the main dilemmas for raising maturity in the application lifecycle. The possibilities for automation gains in recent years have been greatly expanded. Tools such as Docker, Gitlab, Jenkins, among others, increased the capacity of automation to another level, and, as a consequence, gave a boom productivity of the teams.

IDEs have also been responsible for a significant breakthrough in developer productivity, with new features for both coding and integration with the latest tools mentioned.

If we take Zend Studio as an example, we will see that from within the same development environment, we can access and work with the main tools mentioned above, such as Docker, Amazon, and Git. This makes it much easier and allows the developer to do more in less time.

Zend Studio is the Swiss army knife of IDEs for PHP and provides a wide range of possibilities. In addition to Zend Studio, there are several professional IDEs for you to choose from. Netbeans, PHPStorm, and Eclipse with PDT are just a few alternatives. Of course, when you know all the shortcuts of a tool and have mastered how to use it, any change will bring a learning cost. So I see that choosing the IDE for your preference is something very personal. Either way, investing your time and money into knowledge in a professional IDE can bring a high return in the medium to long term.

But when we talk about maintaining and sustaining an environment for critical applications, we have also made several strides.

Automated provisioning tools, such as Puppet and Chef, have revolutionized the market by enabling automatic creation of environments bringing the possibility of resizing the environment in response to a change quickly and securely.

The virtualization tools were the great precursors bringing the possibility of reuse and automate the provisioning of environments. These virtualization solutions, added to the automated provisioning, grew absurdly. And along these lines, Docker brought a new level of professionalism by speeding up and reducing resource consumption even more.

However, when we are talking about PHP, besides performing the deployment of the environment, there are also several other activities to keep PHP up-to-date and secure. Among these activities, the monitoring of the launch of new versions, mainly that corrects bugs identified, is a critical task to ensure the safety and reliability of the environment.

Besides, even if we make sure that we create the environment securely and reliably, we still need to ensure that it stays that way, so in the previous chapter, we have seen how Zend Server can help maintain configuration two environments.

When we say configuration, we are referring to: values in the PHP.ini file, installed extensions .ini files (such as OCI8), application performance threshold settings (response time, memory consumption, between others).

This capability helps ensures that any change is quickly identified and brought up. Also, you can easily choose what you want to do to correct the wrong configuration. You can apply the change identified on one machine to all others, or you can apply the version that is registered to the device that is in the wrong configuration.

In addition, you can export and import settings for environments. This possibility brings high flexibility of configuration management since you can share the configuration or even versioning it and ensure more effective control of configuration management. Imagine that you may be able to version one configuration each time a change is made and thus return to the configuration of a particular moment in the past simply and directly.

These settings can be imported at any time to any server. This capability can be useful both in machine provisioning automation and in upgrading in critical environments that can not be changed and need mechanisms to respond to situations such as those described.

Regarding the work of infrastructure professionals, one of the most time-consuming points is precisely the configuration of the webserver. This activity is often done manually, which ultimately takes a lot of time for the team to create the environment and configure vhost.

With Zend Server, you can centrally manage the virtual host from the application interface. That way, as we saw in Chapter 5, when you make a specific change to the virtual host, you can save it and delegate it to Zend Server to do the same on all servers in the cluster.

That way, you can save a lot of time and, in the same way, offer a more exceptional guarantee of process reliability.

In the next chapter we will address a crucial issue for those who invest in a technology: reliability.

CHAPTER 7 - RELIABILITY

This is one of the key issues for technology decision makers when choosing to invest in PHP. This is because the investment will have a high cost, not only financial, but also and especially energy. Both to overcome the maturity learning curve and to maintain the environment and solution.

Decision makers most concerned about the implications of their long-term choices are often more concerned with the reliability of their decisions.

Professional support to support technology is a crucial issue for adoption in this context. That is why large companies invest a large sum of resources to ensure their customers will be available if they need to.

This is particularly important in a world where the pace of innovation is scary. The decision maker needs to know how reliable the technology in which he is investing.

In this scenario, PHP has a brilliant story. How to evaluate a technology created around an open source with a community so committed and so available?

With 83% of websites on the web, PHP is considered by many to be Internet English, precisely because of its universal availability of professionals, applications and resources.

But often, the corporate market needs more. No more support, but a formal service-level contract with an organization, also formal, that brings to the technology and the investment the formal guarantee necessary for the investment to be possible.

For this reason, Zend was created to bring to the corporate market the professionalism and formal seal that it needs in its projects.

By investing in a solution like Zend Server, an organization is investing in a subscription with a 24x7x365 support network, with a turnaround time for any critical events.

And, more than that, ensuring the reliability of the application environment is also an important thing that Zend has inserted into its solution.

With Zend Server, any changes made to your application environment are properly recorded and documented. If someone changes the value of a configuration or even deploys a new version, you will have an audit trail that will log all changes in the environment.

This is reliability. It's ensuring that your investment is protected by a professional support team and that your investment will protect everyone else, which is what happens with the Audit Trail.

You can always count on the community, but with Zend Server you will have a time-of-service agreement to support your operation. We know that, in many cases, we also need face-to-face support, so at ETTBrasil we have created our professional services unit to support companies at these times. And we are sharing our role model so that you can also support your organization in any of your decisions.

In addition, you can also count on the LTS. The PHP lifecycle brings a clear roadmap of evolution and it is very important to ensure that you are within the current life cycle of security patches. If you are using a version that is no longer supported, you may be exposed to any new vulnerabilities that are discovered.

It is always better to make progress by seeking benefits rather than risk avoidance. I am sure that evolving the PHP version of your application will bring great benefits, but if you have an unsupported version, I recommend that you do it as urgently as possible to avoid being vulnerable to any potential attack.

All the advice above is valid for any web server or PHP version you are using. However, for those who use Zend Server, Zend has also prepared more support for this scenario. The LTS, or Long-Term Support . With LTS, you are guaranteed Zend's support for creating PHP bug fixes in previous versions for a period of time, even after the formal support coverage of the PHP community has closed.

This may help you gain more time to migrate from an earlier version of your application to a new version, but do not let it put you in a comfort zone. Migrate as quickly as possible, you will see the benefits.

To support you in your migration, you can use tools like CodeSniffer and / or PHP 7 Express (built into Zend Studio). These tools will perform a static analysis of your code and can give a quick diagnosis of how prepared your application is for migration. Anyway, by putting the new version in the air, you still need tools to monitor your application and give you the ability to respond quickly, as we saw in the chapter on diagnosing errors. With these tools, you will be able to migrate with greater confidence.

In the next chapter we will address one of my favorite subjects: software architecture.

CHAPTER 8 - ARCHITECTURE
CONSIDERATIONS

The architecture of your system is how you solved the problem
that your application needs to address. In many cases, we see in the
market architects being restricted to say which framework and the
database that will be used.

The problem, when we start the project choosing the
framework and the database, is that we are creating a bad
marriage. Marriage with the technology of things that should and
will evolve.

We see many organizations stuck in old technologies because
they first chose which frameworks and databases they would use.

So we see the framework engineers always thinking of evolving,
while those programmers who started by choosing the database
and the frameworks remain stuck with their choices.

In some cases, this is detrimental to the progress of the project.

Okay, but then how will we do when we have a
problem? Typically, the choice to start a project by choosing the
framework and database is a view that the system will do nothing
more than provide an interface for presentation and data
collection, whereas what matters is the database.

It may be a good choice for those who will use the data directly
for intelligence analysis, but certainly not for those who will use the
system. And, especially, for those who will build, maintain, and
evolve the system for years to come.

For these, the database is the last of the concerns. Most programmers do not even have access to the data model. And that's okay. What they need to have is straightforward access and control of the class model. That, yes, is gold.

As programmers, we need to understand that what we do will be used by others in the future and, especially, must be maintained by others in the organization.

This conception makes it easy to understand that the vision of creating a system is nothing more than a graphical interface to the system; you will have to reevaluate your decision.

During my career, I found, at various times, projects that stucked in choices made around databases and frameworks. Those choices made maintenance and evolution more difficult

If you consider, for example, applications that have been made in MVC frameworks and used the app primarily for the bridge between the user interface and the database, you will find that it will be tough to evolve that application without a substantial rewrite.

So how to do it? The output is the valuation of your domain classes. Start with them. Try to solve the problem that your application aims to solve with domain classes directly, and defer to the maximum the choice for the database and framework.

Of course, you will have to opt for these technologies at some point. Still, when you start with domain classes, you will be strengthening a reasonably reusable part of your application. With technologies like composer (and the SATIS package repository), you can maintain a class asset that will allow you to evolve into new frameworks with low rewriting of the critical part of your application.

I'm confident that the engineers behind frameworks also might think like that. Solve your business problems with your domain classes, then, plug it into the framework for a fast and secure development. Try to keep all business logic in the domain so you will be free to evolve togheter with the frameworka and database technology.

We have come to the end of the main topics of our conversation, in the next chapter I will make the final considerations.

FINAL CONSIDERATIONS

In this book, we cover several important topics for your company to have a better return on your PHP investments. However, we are far from closing the discussion. I think we're just getting started.

The relationships between developers and infrastructure (DevOps) gain new contours and potentialities every day. New tools make different forms of work and relationships viable. Some startups are already structured around agile methodologies of product creation and development.

The continuous evolution of computer processing power and the speed of PHP inspires us to imagine the new frontiers that can be exploited by language, such as Big Data analysis and Artificial Intelligence, among others.

Every day, we see new features being created in tools aimed at programmers, to provide capabilities to increase their productivity and help to identify and correct errors more easily.

Cloud computing is becoming increasingly accessible, allowing for ever more easy computing capabilities. It will enable you to have a technical ability to scale virtually unlimited.

It is also worth highlighting the multiplication of sources and forms of knowledge transmission. Videos, courses, webinars, and a wide range of new formats allow professionals to have access to the information necessary for their evolution. The new knowledge, coupled with work methodologies and tools, will allow an exponential advance of professional productivity.

Issues of reliability also become increasingly relevant issues. In addition to regulations on data security and concerns about leaks, these concerns are no longer just issues that permeate the technology sector and become core issues for organizations.

It's impossible to have a clear vision of what is to come. We can only look a little further on the reality in which we live. But one thing is sure: people and organizations working with PHP have a leading role in building our future.

I hope this book has been able to inspire you to continue your journey and, together, move forward in our mission to create applications that change the way we live and how we relate.

www.ingramcontent.com/pod-product-compliance
Lightning Source LLC
LaVergne TN
LVHW041221050326
832903LV00021B/730